Millionaire Mind Programming

Millionaire Mind Programming
Unlock Your Hidden Inner Millionaire

John Alexander

Millionaire Mind Programming

Copyright © Nuday
1st Edition 2008
2nd Edition 2009
3rd Edition 2022

ALL RIGHTS RESERVED. No part of this book may be reproduced or transmitted for resale or use by any party other than the individual purchaser who is the sole authorized user of this information. All other reproduction or transmission, in any form or by any means, electronic or mechanical, including photocopying, recording or by any informational storage or retrieval method, is prohibited without express written permission from John Alexander.

The author may be contacted at his Website
www.JohnAlexander.com

Published by Nuday Productions
Printed in the USA

Contents

Preface	3
CHAPTER 1	5
From Rags to Riches	5
CHAPTER 2	13
Success Begins Where Worry Ends	13
CHAPTER 3	17
Negative Survival Programming (NSP)	17
Parental NSP	20
CHAPTER 4	23
What Success is NOT	23
CHAPTER 5	30
Defining Yourself First	30
CHAPTER 6	34
Define Your Mind,	34
And Your Mind Defines You	34
CHAPTER 7	42
How the Mind Works	42
CHAPTER 8	46
How to Program the Mind	46
Programming for Millionaire Status	50
CHAPTER 9	54
Preventing Failure	54
CHAPTER 10	58
3 KEYS TO SUCCESS	58
CHAPTER 11	60

It Happens in Three's 60
CHAPTER 12 62
The Success Cycle 62
    BE DO HAVE 64
CHAPTER 13 68
How to Begin any Success Cycle 68
CHAPTER 14 74
Affirmation Programming 74
The Trilogy of Affirmations 80
CHAPTER 15 81
On Cause and Effect 82
CHAPTER 16 87
25 Secrets That Will 87
Explode Your Business 87
Chapter 17 96
The Key to Helping Your Client Achieve All their Dreams 96
CHAPTER 18 98
Leverage Your Way Up 98
CHAPTER 19 104
Putting it all Together 104
Final Thoughts 106
Is This Your Defining Moment? 107
Books by John Alexander 110
About the Author 120

Preface

What is it that makes some people successful and financially secure in their life while others seem to just limp along in life? I spent a life-time learning the secrets found in this book. I have pulled information from both my own experiences as well as by observing the many clients I have taught and learned from over the years.

In this book, I will reveal those secrets I have discovered that turned me and many of my coaching clients into the top people in their industries. You can apply this to your own business too.

There is a certain way of conditioning the mind that can bring you that which you desire. We'll call this conditioning – Mind Programming. Mind Programming is the art of developing your hidden INNER MILLIONAIRE.

When I understood the mind programming techniques found in this book, I started living my life with new understanding that completely changed my financial situation, so can you.

Over and over, I have seen the same thing happen to clients that have purchased my courses, or attended my webinars or become Coaching Clients. In the following pages you will find those same key principles you can use to become a millionaire.

CHAPTER 1

From Rags to Riches

I'll begin by sharing my own journey from failure to millionaire through understanding certain unchanging Keys to Success and the Mind Programs that made those accomplishments possible.

In the late 1980's the real estate market had turned bad, I found myself with no job, no money, no home, and a feeling that even if I built back up to success, something else would just take it away again.

This resulted in lost hope. At that point, even though I had been previously semi-successful in real estate investing, I was now no longer "ready for success" due to negative mind programs which I ran as a reaction to the current negative events which I was experiencing.

There's a point in most of our lives where you will have your defining moment. It happens in an instant. It happens in a second. You will never forget what you are doing or where you are at when it happens. Everything will just come together and you will realize that you have to make a change in your life. You will find that you have to do it now and that there is no going back.

I was living and sleeping on the street. I found myself begging for change on the street, just to eat.

For me, my defining moment came at my lowest point. I was literally living and begging on the streets of Las Vegas. At night, I slept next to a dumpster behind Bally's Casino and between cars in nearby apartment parking lots, anywhere that felt safe.

One day, after months of living like this, I didn't care that I hadn't raised enough money to pay the cost of the $1.99 house special where I ate every night. At that point, I went over to St Vincent's homeless shelter, just north of downtown to get a free meal.

They handed out sandwiches that evening. I was sitting on a curb outside the shelter next to other homeless people. As I was about to take a bite of the sandwich, I froze in place. I just stared at this chicken salad sandwich, knowing that if I took a bite, I would continue down the wrong path, down the wrong road. I was going to quit life; I was probably going to die. I knew this was the wrong road, and in that second, it hit me and I made the decision. I dropped the sandwich and everything that eating it would have really meant.

I never took the first bite. I stood up, and made the decision to take my life in a new direction, I didn't know how yet, but I knew this was not the right one. That was my defining moment, a moment we all get to at some point when things aren't going in the right direction and we must do something to change direction altogether. We all remember these kinds of rebirth type of moments when they happen. It's a combination of a deep emotional experience combined with a intentional new direction that flips in the mind like a switch. It's a rebirth.

If you want to live life to the fullest and gain financial independence, you too will have to drop the sandwich, "the crumbs the world provides." To do this, you will need to drop your previous mind programming that is deciding your life for you at this time. You are about to learn that your mind is the only thing that can turn your life into something great.

In my journey from broke to my first million, I learned it was negative mind programming that I had to discard. I learned that it was new programming that I would have to install. It wasn't about having a job or starting a business, it was all about what I programmed myself to BE. When I was homeless and had nothing, it was because I told myself I was homeless and had nothing. I told others that and they acknowledged and reinforced it by giving me change or a sandwich. As such, I earned a beggar's wage and lived a beggar's life.

In seeking a new direction. Someone I trusted had told me a homeless person could get a job at one of the local car washes. I believed this person and applied for the job. I got a job vacuuming car at a local carwash in Las Vegas. I became a person who worked and continued for some time, to work at a carwash. I did this because I believed and unknowingly programmed my mind by saying "I could work at a carwash." As such, I ...earned a car wash attendant's wage.

Over the next few years, I had moved on from the car wash back into real estate, but without the success I was looking to achieve. I made just enough to cover a typical month-to-month living.

I continued in this circle until I met a mentor that exposed the mental cycle in which I was caught. The next phase of my mindset education. I learned that I was defining who I was at any given time. I learned that I was programming myself to be what I was even before I got there. I also learned that there is a way to reprogram my mind. I took some of the exercises he recommended and expanded them over the next five years into what worked best for me and eventually for my clients.

I have detailed them in this book along with other important information that helped me program myself my ideal life, and which can help you do the same.

A Millionaire isn't Always a Millionaire in Terms of Money?

But keep in mind it is not always about becoming a millionaire in terms of a dollars. A Dollar is something of value, an idea is also something of value. One idea could be a million dollar idea. That idea makes you a millionaire.

Your millionaire mind set may be in valued in in family, it may be helping a charity, it may be in becoming the artist you dreamed of. Your definition of millionaire is uniquely yours. Millionaire is really your Desire that has a value attached to it. It has many labels, like Success, Happy Marriage, Health. It just this book narrows it down to using money and success as the goal but the process here can be used to or modified to achieve the values you seek in any part of your life.

What makes the difference between somebody who becomes successful and somebody who doesn't? I'll detail exactly what I have seen that sets the two apart. One way gets you on a track to wealth and success, the other on a track destined for failure.

It is a blending of programming your mind and understanding the keys to attaining success that will allow you to succeed in the accumulation of wealth.

I've made a lot of money over the years, literally millions and millions of dollars. I've accumulated that by following the steps found in this book. But I had to learn them the hard way. I had to learn over a long period of time through experimentation to determine what worked and what did not, costing me valuable time and money. You don't have to learn them the way I did, because I am giving you a lifetime of learning exactly how to become a millionaire.

During my early years, I did not earn as much as I could have. What I read in books seemed great but did not really work. Still, I never stopped trying to find the missing pieces to the "Success Puzzle." Eventually, I did and now so have you.

I hope I can shorten the process for you so you can accumulate money a lot quicker than I did. I believe you can do what some of my other clients have done by getting on a fast track to becoming a millionaire.

Through many years of trial and error during the 1990's, I discovered unique "mental systems" and "business systems" for achieving success and anyone can use the same processes once you learn them.

I know that sounds too good to be true. Which is something else we are about to examine in a moment. Yet, it happened to me and is happening to others that use these techniques and methods.

If they can do it, so can you. With that said, you may be ready to do the work, give up the time, focus and devote your life to achieving what you truly desire. Since you purchased this book, that desire is to become a millionaire.

While this book will concentrate on financial achievement, you can use the techniques for achieving any goal you set for yourself. With these techniques you can find the right mate, find your dream job, achieve fame, travel the world, or accomplish whatever you want to become. You can use these same techniques to coach others into doing the same.

This book will show you exactly how to become a millionaire or achieve your dreams using a set of specific mind programming techniques. Techniques you can use to achieve massive success in anything.

[12]

CHAPTER 2

Success Begins Where Worry Ends

"The best way of becoming a millionaire is by helping others become millionaires."

Any lifestyle you desire can be achieved by programming the correct content into the core of your being... your mind.

The world gives you just enough to survive, but your mind can give you a fulfilled and "rich" lifestyle.

I became ready for success and started on a journey that took me to multi-millionaire status in just a few years after learning how to program my mind. I then started to share with others how they could do the same and have continued doing so since.

I still have concerns and challenges... just like everyone else, but no longer do I have the same kind of worries. I came to the understanding that losing everything and coming back from nothing could be repeated again if needed. So why worry?

This is the key to understanding how not to worry about the future events that may or may not come. The understanding that we all started with nothing at birth and could do it all over again should the worst happen is not really realized by those who never lost, at least once in life.

Financial worries are caused by believing that you cannot come back from (or replace) a loss. For most people, what they lose then defines who they see themselves as. What you lose will define what you no longer need and was just getting in your way.

Coming back from such a loss can come with a giant bonus... you actually get more or attain to a higher position when coming back from a total loss. You usually become a better and stronger person unless you continue to blame others for your previous loss. Most people define themselves by what they have or what they have lost ...or who they are in their peer group or by their partner in life. None of these define who we are, but we can think, thus believe, they do.

Your mind programming defines who you are, who you will be, what you will have, and what you will not have.

By starting out with nothing, you tend to be willing to RISK more. By risking more, you gain more. Risk is always accompanied by some degree of worry of loss. It's those who worry excessively over losses who will tend never to risk enough to attain true wealth or financial security in life. Just as a married person must risk divorce, so to you will risk to achieve the success you desire.

Over the years I have seen client after client go from having little or worse, being upside down, to earning millions of dollars. There is no reason why you can't do the same thing if you follow the concepts contained in these pages.

I want to share one of the great stories that unfolded in Charles K.'s life. Charles was one of my first clients that became a millionaire using my real estate techniques. Before getting into my coaching sessions, Charles was a security guard and had gotten himself fired from his job. He was absolutely down financially, but not mentally, he had no money left at all and lived with his mother.

He scraped together enough money to invest in my program and started attending my weekly coaching sessions. His home-based business suddenly he took off. Within a matter of two months, he had made over $8,000.00 in profits from his first two deals. His programming had accepted that he could make much more than a security guard's salary, but his mother's mind programming hadn't yet.

Even faced with holding the checks in her hands, she didn't believe the checks were real. She wadded them up and threw them on the floor. Well, the checks were real and there were to be a lot more of them to come. Charles went on to earn millions in his career. Charles and I continue to this day to share a connection that can never be broken because when you have each other's backs in the trenches, that friendship is for life.

Not a week goes by these days when I don't hear amazing success stories from those that I have helped unlock the doors that are usually never entered by most because they were never given the keys.

CHAPTER 3

Negative Survival Programming (NSP)

We all have default mind programs running in our mind that I call "Survival Programs". There is positive as well as negative survival programs that determine our current state of being. Negative Survival Programming or (NSP). This is the type of mind program that keeps 95% of the population "just getting by". NSP is what becomes programmed into your mind from your environment, friends, family and peers which then creates negative effects in your life.

It determines how you see, feel, and react to events in your life. It also draws events to you and pushes you toward certain events. Negative survival programs keep you pulled down instead of allowing you to rise above situations. It keeps drawing the same issues into your life so you repeat what you already have going on in your life.

Early man would only concern himself with the way and means of finding the next meal and ensuring that he had protection from the environment. Today, most people still operate on this type of programming. "I only have enough money to live month-to-month" "I must remain at my job as it is my only source of income/benefits."

This leads a person to only concentrating on the short-term goals of weekly or monthly survival issues. They trade all their available time and effort for making sure they have "enough" to get by for now.

Other NSP has been placed in our minds by others influencing us or through repetition. How many times have you heard "If it is too good to be true, it probably is." Yet, there are many things that happen to all of us that are too good to be true. Winning the lottery is too good to be true, finding the love of your life is too good to be true, and winning a lawsuit is too good to be true. You can't argue with the fact that there are some things that happen to us that are too good to be true as well as situations that don't work out. It's not because situations are too good to be true, but because they just didn't work out for us at the time.

If a person uses a system and becomes rich, then another person can use the same or similar "too good to be true" method to become rich. However, another person may use the same system and not become rich. It has nothing to do with the system; it has everything to do with what you believe to be true, how your mind is programmed.

A common NSP that you could be running and keeping you from becoming a millionaire is that you believe it is "too good to be true."

Can you do it? Of course, you can. You will shortly learn how to remove this program and any other that is stopping you from achieving your financial destination. Let's look at two very common NSP that are affecting millions of people since the recession started.

Since the Recession of 2008, you could be running a NSP called, "I can't get rich during a recession" or "It's not right to get rich during a recession." Or even worse, "The 1% rich are bad. It's morally wrong to be wealthy." Today, more than anytime in the past, Religions, political parties, corporations, and the media are promoting that it is morally wrong to be wealthy.

Their propaganda is programming an entire generation to live on crumbs while they get wealthier. None of them are telling you to not spend your money with them. They think that if you don't get wealthy, then there is more for them. That is wrong, of course, but they don't have an abundance attitude, they have a zero-sum belief. The belief that if one person loses an amount, then another person must gain that same amount and visa-versa, a false theory in the wealth accumulation game.

It doesn't matter what the economy is doing, or where you live. As the USSR collapsed financially back in the 80's, there were more millionaires made in that country than in all its history. One of the largest numbers of individual millionaires created in America before the present time came out of the 1929 Great Depression. In 1982, Mexico was in an economic collapse amid runaway inflation, interest rates and debt defaults (sound familiar?). Even the boldest investors were bailing out. Carlos Slim Helú, a Mexican business man, kept buying up assets at panic prices. Carlos Slim Helú became at one time, the wealthiest man in the world. He employed over 200,000 people across Mexico.

The wealthy individuals that are created in down economies are the very people who give jobs to the poorly programmed people and help them get back to a decent feeling of stability. Therefore, not only is it right to become rich during recessions and depressions, it's the only thing that is being done right for everyone else in the country. You owe it to your fellow man to become rich during these times and to help them as well as yourself and your own family.

Everyone that follows the principals and methods I reveal in these pages can develop a millionaire's mindset. Once you BEGIN something, and by not STOPPING, you will succeed. Most people are afraid to begin and those that do will give up and stop too soon. Not beginning at all or beginning then stopping too early are major reasons for failure.

Many people won't even attempt to start a business of their own because should they fail, they fear looking like a failure to their family, their peers, and friends. That kind of fear is a NSP.

Parental NSP

Most parents will program their children not to take risks like starting a business or getting that sale commission-only job. It's not that they don't want you to succeed, it's they don't like to see you fail. They feel responsible for both your successes and failures. It can also make them feel bad to see you feel the pain of failure. As parents, it's actually their job to protect you from anything negative. Understanding this explains a lot about children raised by overly cautious parents.

From a baby, they start programming their children not to do this or that, survival skills. At first, that helps a child survive, but only up to the level of where the parents started meeting their own failures in life and where they stopped taking certain risks. Where parents start to caution you not to do something you see other's doing and succeeding at, is often the point where they can no longer be your mentor. This is the point where you need to find another mentor that has surmounted this new set of possible failures, and even excelled. Then use their knowledge to continue your climb on the ladder of success.

Just knowing you might have NSP running will help you stop and ask yourself what influence does my family and peers have on me making this decision. Stop reading right now and write down what NSP are you running that would be along these lines?

_____
_____
_____
_____
_____
_____

Ask yourself, do I have a life-long pattern of outside programming that would lead me to make a DEFAULT decision here. If your parents (one or both) have always leaned toward the "Don't Risk It" camp, then you know you may have more work cut out for you.

You have a system here to follow that will help you achieve success as you define it. You can use this system to program your mind to achieve any goal.

Becoming a millionaire is a mental game first and a physical game second. When you have the basic understanding of what it is that makes a person successful, as well as what to avoid that attracts a failed or stagnate life; then you will be ready to join the ranks of the truly financially successful.

CHAPTER 4

What Success is NOT

Let's first look at what success is NOT. Many people think success requires LUCK. I'm sure you have heard this saying – "You've got to be in the right place at the right time." But in reality, every place is the right place at the right time. We just don't see that fact because we have a NSP running that looks for problems and shuts us down when they appear.

We all are in a constant state of the same luck. In fact, every event that happens to a person happens with an equal amount of luck or probability. A bad event happening in your life doesn't equal bad luck. Just as a good event occurring in your life doesn't mean that it came as a result of good luck. It's all a matter of probability, given the number of attempts with the right amount of knowledge.

The problem most people have with bad events is they don't see them with a clear mind. Because of this, they don't act on them so the opportunity hidden in the bad event just fizzle away as a non-event. Or worse, they lead to more bad events. When I lost everything, I saw that as a streak of bad luck, yet it is the very thing that opened my eyes to discover the secret that gave me great wealth, happiness and peace of mind.

What I perceived as my bad luck was actually just a bad event which helped lead me to the right path. As you can see, there really is no such thing as bad luck or good luck. There are just events that come into being which we see as bad or good due to our current mind programming which attributes the cause of the event to "luck." When you are shut down in one area of your life due to events, refocus onto another area. I assure you that you have areas of your life that are just waiting to blossom but so far have not because your focus was elsewhere.

Nothing bad happens to the wise person, only a learning experience, a redirection, refocus, and new planning. When something negative shuts you down, ask yourself what other thing have you been putting off that has potential. What other event or dream did you sideline while things were going so smoothly?

When you become confused from bad events, don't automatically try new things, go back to what you know, something from your past, basics that were working and just modify things. Switching to something brand new should only be done when things are going well and you can afford to gamble on new and unproven directions.

Fortunes will come and go for most wealthy people, attaining it is one thing, keeping it is another. But knowing that you can attain it over and over because you know how to run correct mind programs will keep you from letting a total loss blow you out of the game.

The market crash of 2008 blew a lot of millionaires out of the water, they found themselves dragging to the shore with just enough energy not to have drowned but no money left. That was no time to cry, no time to say the party is over. That was a time to refocus. Find another entry point in the game of money accumulation. It was an opportunity to help others just like you that lost so much. The most successful didn't start over with a entirely new direction, they just rebuilt the now broken system they had already been doing.

For many, depression or negativity sets in when you risk and lose it all, or when you don't have a starting point you feel comfortable with. Most depression caused by "events" are just a mindset issue and can be reprogrammed with a little time for replanting and restarting a business. When people normally in control of every part of their life and business suffers a lost, they shut down, they stop. This leads to depression and depression leads to a new mind program that continues the path in the wrong direction. The solution is to make a new plan and make a lot of little changes to what was working.

Once you have a plan and see a little success, you will find that you can soar back to where you left off within a minimum of time. Studies have shown that millionaires that have lost it all from some unexpected event will regain it all plus more within just a few short years. It's like riding a bicycle.

Never fear that you will lose it all, be willing to risk everything as you begin your journey, temper the risk as you gain more, but still be willing to risk. That thing you refocus onto after any bad beat down is going to involve taking a whole new level of risk. Be willing to risk it all at the start, that's because you have nothing to lose at that point. You just think you have something to lose, but those things you think you have left… you will lose for sure if you don't take the risk. So, in fact, you have nothing to lose by risking it all.

Each event can also lead to another depending on the mind program you have running. In other words, even when a great opportunity presents itself, if a person is not ready to see it and act on it, then nothing will happen, it becomes a NON-EVENT.

Indecision always leads to inaction and inaction always leads to less, not more of something. Your enemy is being undecided. Indecision is how you stay in the same place. You can't advance without risking a bad decision. You will make bad decisions and you will always recover, but fear of making a bad decision keeps you from ever making good decisions. If you really think about it, you will discover that your really don't make that many bad decisions. That's because even when you did, what happened afterwards lead to something good at some point. Your mind erases bad decision outcomes because all decisions lead to something good at some point.

How many times have you heard someone say they had been in prison and that was the best thing that ever happened to them because otherwise they'd be dead now? That's because the bad decisions that lead them there was topped by the good that came with a reflective understanding at a later time. But you can't see that in the moments of failure. It's a future you that you must tell your current you that this will pass and things will be even better in the near future.

Therefore, all decisions you make will be right for you, good or bad. Making them is the key because not making them doesn't allow you to advance. Advancement in life and on your road to success and millions always begin with making a decision about something. Now that you know you can't make the wrong decision, start making decisions now.

If decision making is required to get you on the road to success, then making more decisions will help you get there faster and easier. Look for them, they are all around you if you look for them. What can you say "yes" or "no" to. The more you do the more focused your journey becomes. That's right some decisions mean you say no to them.

There are two parts to every decision, making the **Decision** and then taking **Action**. After every decision is made, an action is going to be required. This the where most people hit their first wall of resistance. That's because taking action is where you actually have something at risk. Actions always come with risk and the bigger the risk, the more important it is that you take the action required. This is because big rewards only come from big risks.

Once you decide to buy something you know you want or need, you now have to pull out your cash and put it on the line. If you don't follow through, then you really never made the decision. If you can't pull the trigger on the action, that tells you that you failed to make a decision to begin with.

If you find yourself failing to make decisions or fail to follow through with action, then ask yourself what NSP's could you have running that are making you react this way. What in the past hurt so bad that it made you freeze at one or both these points? So many times, it was a bad event that isn't very hard to find and erase. Other times, it's an adopted belief from others.

You can elect to see bad events as a process to a good event. There are no real losses in life, just steps to great things and great events. Release yourself of thinking in terms of good or bad luck and see every event, good or bad as a stepping stone to a GREAT EVENT in your future. Realize you can make decisions and carry through with required actions to get you what and where you want in life.

We fear loss more than the desire for gain. Fear causes us not to make decisions, not to take action, not to risk a loss. Fear keeps you frozen in place. Fear is just a chemical in your brain that your mind produced due to your current mind programming. You can't advance if fear rules your life. Of course, some fear is healthy and keeps us alert to obvious losses like a snake bite. But fear must be examined against NSP.

Determining what is good or bad is based on how we see events and things. We filter all situations through a predetermined set of rules and expectations pre-programmed into our mind.

We view everything through a filter we created in our mind. These filters can be changed.

Just as your eyes would see everything in the color red if you wore rose colored glasses, your mind sees opportunity that presents itself through a filter you currently have in place in your mind; put there through your current mind programming.

The good news is that you can manipulate this filter based on how you see yourself in relationship to the world around you.

Everything you see through your mind will be viewed from the context of WHO you are; WHAT you are; HOW you are; and WHERE you are in relation to the issue at hand. The program that is running in your mind creates the Who, What, Where, and How you are, and can be altered at any time by simply reprogramming the "BEING" (Mind) part of you.

The "Being" part of you is how you define yourself in your environment and to the people around. You have decided or allowed yourself to BE someone. That person can be defined by looking at the parts of what makes up the "Being" part of you.

By looking and defining the following, you can begin to see what types of NSP you are running that are keeping you from success.

CHAPTER 5

Defining Yourself First

Who, What, How, and Where you are, are defined by how you see yourself and see your place in the world. You must understand this before you can achieve/have anything.

You can see some of your current programming by asking yourself the following questions. Write the answers in this book after each question. It is important that you answer them before reading further.

1. Are you lucky or unlucky?
2. Are you rich, poor, or just broke?
3. Are you happy, sad, bored, or apathetic?
4. Are you a millionaire? Do you think you will become a millionaire?
5. Are you from a problem family and that is the cause of your current condition?
6. Do you keep getting "burned" in financial areas?
7. Do you lack a proper education to attain success?
8. Do you seem to be taking two steps forward and one step back?
9. Do you feel "trapped" in your current job due to financial responsibilities or lack of knowledge?

10. Are you afraid to fail and does it make you feel bad to fail? Do you fear "looking" like a failure to your friends/peers and family?

11. Do you find yourself thinking a lot about past failures? Does it cause anxiety? Does it prevent you from changing your current situation by accepting the risks that go along with the change?

12. Do you find yourself talking to some other person (other than your spouse) about making important decisions?

13. Can you MAKE things work even when they don't seem to be working so well?

14. What groups do you belong to and what are their requirements of your behavior and thought patterns?

15. How well do you take criticism?

By answering these questions, you will begin to see a person you may not recognize as who you really want to be.

Others will be fine with their answers to these questions but will not realize how some of these answers are actually holding you back from achieving financial success.

For purposes of this book and the concept of becoming wealthy, the most important question above, relates to WHO you are. It is how you SEE yourself in terms of poor, broke, rich, or millionaire.

Define yourself in relation to the issue you face. In order to discover the NSP that is keeping you from achieving your goal, ask yourself this question. ***"What exactly is stopping me from taking the next step toward my goal?"*** Write these issues down on paper. These are the NSP's and beliefs your mind is making true in your life. You will learn how to destroy these debilitating survival programs in Chapter 14.

"Being a millionaire is a mindset, not a bank account. Create the millionaire mind first, then the bank account comes automatically."

Achieving success means you will fail over and over on the journey. We all fail in only two ways. We fail forwards or we fail backwards. Failing forwards keeps you in the right direction to success.

CHAPTER 6

Define Your Mind,
And Your Mind Defines You

Your reality and how you define yourself as who you are in this moment determines your immediate and near-term prospects of success. Reality is your mind's interpretation of what is real and true right now based on what your mind has been programmed to accept as existing.

If you see yourself as broke, then that is who you DEFINE yourself to BE and success cannot be achieved until re-programming occurs.

Your mind always works to create the results of what it believes exists. Whether it is actually real or true is not at issue in the mind. This mind's acceptance of this Existence is called a Belief. Your reality is created by your mind's beliefs.

If you are broke today, it's because you were originally programmed as such by determining that you are broke thus, the mind made this your reality. It made it true whether it was true or not. A person earning $100 a month may believe that anyone earning $5,000 a month is rich and that they themselves are broke.

Some people are earning $5,000 a month but spend it all monthly. They may say they are broke because their mind is telling them that they have no money left at the end of the month, thus broke. Their mind equates no savings and spending all their income as being broke.

Your mind will keep making your current situation true so you never succeed financially. So, whether you have an income of $100 a month, $5,000 a month, or $20,000 a month, your mind has already been given orders to keep you in your current month-to-month survival status by making your program true.

Even if you increase your income, your mind will make you spend the extra increase until you are "broke" again. You can't help it until your mind programming is changed.

Nobody truly starts out as being broke or poor. We all start out in the same state at the time of our birth, having nothing and not being negative. No one can define a newborn as broke; maybe the parents are, but not the newborn. As children, we are then programmed by our parents, our peers, society, and our own acceptance of these mind programs which define who and what we are.

Over the years, as circumstances change, we continue to redefine who we are by our current circumstances and beliefs. This is like being who you are by accident.

If we are not able to find work due to circumstances outside our control; we define ourselves as poor. Once we get a job, the program is still running and we spend all of our monthly income so we are broke again. We may also find a reason to quit or get ourselves fired and we are poor again. Thus, some people live month-to-month on any given income, or go from job-to-job, or not even bother looking for a job, all due to their poor mind programming.

Many of us have an NSP running that says we must find a new job... even though you may be living in a city with extreme unemployment, and instead, you should be looking to starting your own business with a customer base outside your city or even outside your state. But your programming forces you into its predefined box of "job" equals "survival."

We create in our life, what our mind has been programmed to expect and it defines who and what we are.

Here are the basic NSP's that people are running that keeps them from success and true wealth:

- I'll never become a millionaire
- I'm not a millionaire
- I'm not worthy of being a *millionaire*
- I don't deserve to become wealthy
- I'm broke
- I'm poor
- I'm uneducated so I can't become successful
- I'm too old to start a business or new career
- I hate selling
- I can't sell
- This business model doesn't work
- If I start a business, it's just going to fail
- I can't catch a break
- I can't change
- I'll never have what I want
- For every step I take forward, I take two steps back
- I'm unlucky in business
- People don't respect me
- I'm a victim (been hurt, scammed, etc.)
- I'm dumb. I'm a failure
- I'm not confident
- I'm going to fail anyway, why try
- I'm afraid I could get sued/fired/hurt
- Why do bad things always happen to me
- That is too hard or too big a project for me
- I need to think about this longer before acting
- My mate is holding me back
- I'm handicapped so I can't…
- I feel I'm going to die soon

- Accepting negative input from family and friends
- I don't what my family/friends see me fail
- Believing that people will not accept you if you do something unusual or different
- Believing opinions when facts differ on the subject
- I failed at that before so I won't try it again
- I will quite if it doesn't work out fast
- I don't want the responsibility that comes with being rich
- I feel guilty being rich
- I'm too young… or too old

Whatever we define ourselves to be, our mind will focus only on things that continue to make that programming true unless we examine it and ask ourselves the questions about that program until we can believe it is a false belief.

Each of the above statements are beliefs, even if subconsciously in our minds that will prevent you from becoming wealthy. To break them, you have to ask yourself how are you manifesting each of these in your mind. This is the process to understanding how much of each of these common beliefs you are running as a default program. To do this, you must drill down using "why" and "how" type questions about each of these basic NSP then follow up with a "is this true" question in order to release them from your existing programming.

Example: Why do I believe for "every step I take forward, I take two backwards?" "Because this or that has happened to me in the past (exact events). But then have I taken 1 step forward and didn't take two back? Yes, I have. Here, and there"... look at exact events. Then finish with... "so, is it always true that If I take one step forward, I will always take two steps back? No, it's not true." In that instant, that NSP program is dead. We will explore one other method later for killing such programming with a question of "have other people overcome that, because if they did, then so can I."

As simple as this sounds. It's something that has to be done, one belief at a time, and it must be addressed in a meditative state of mind in order to rid the NSP. Your full concentration and full attention must be focused on it in order to rid your mind of it.

Don't just read through this list and say yes, I agree that should be something that is a block to me. It is far too embedded in your mind to rid yourself of without a full 10-20 minutes or more spent on each of these beliefs to rid them from your mind. It will take weeks to do this as you should only do one per day to allow your mind to continue to work subconsciously, the remainder of the day with just that one belief as the focus for that day.

You may also have additional beliefs unique to you that you must use the same technique on to rid those as well. Ask yourself why or what is holding you back. Ask yourself at what point in any process you are trying to make work that you find stops that process. That is where you will find your unique NSP that is hindering you that must be addressed.

Finally, once you have rid them, they can slowly creep back in over time and you have to readdress them to keep them out. Understand, your mind never truly forgets anything, including your NSP's. You just neutralize them using these methods. So, if they arise again, you can simply break them apart again using the same technique.

At this point, that NSP has been neutralized, but there is a void there that must be filled, if it isn't filled with some new programming, the old NSP can and often will slip back in to fill it. This is why we now fill that void with what is normally the opposite of what we just ripped out. In our example above using the one step forward two steps back, we would now say, "For every step forward, I take, I have two additional steps that open up, taking me even further." If you are reprogramming the "I'm afraid of looking like a failure to my family/friends" NSP, your replacement might be, even if I failed, my family/friends will support me and encourage me to keep trying. Just flip it and meditate for a while on the new program to instill it and let it float there the rest of the day.

[41]

CHAPTER 7

How the Mind Works

Our mind contains hard-wired programming and soft-wired programming. We can change the soft-wired programming, but not the hard-wired programming.

Our mind is hard-wired from birth. Its sole purpose is to help us survive as a living being. It keeps us alive by working within the environmental rules it believes are true based on previous programs that worked at keeping us alive and safe thus far.

Part of keeping us alive and safe is our ability to adapt to environmental changes. The mind allows itself to be soft-wire programmed through events or input from our thinking mind. Once a new adaptation in our life occurs, it accepts it as a part of reality and then continues to make it part of our lives to keep us alive and safe. This then becomes hard-wire programming which creates reality for us by operating our life through the soft-wired filter place in our minds; a filter you, others, or the environment programmed into existence.

Where and what you are right now was brought into existence by the hard-wire programming running the soft-wired programs running in your mind.

The hard-wired programming mandates the acceptance and the creation of any soft-wired programming we allow to be added at any time during our lifetime. For example, we soft-wire program our mind by believing we are broke, or that we are rich, or that we are a millionaire. Your mind accepts this as true and seeks to create the reality for your life based on this soft-wired programming.

In order to become a millionaire, you must first BE a millionaire in your mind.

In order to become a millionaire, you must program your mind so that it sees itself as a millionaire before you actually get to that status… in order to work towards, and make that programming true; you must get your mind to accept that programming as true. Running the program over and over will convince the hard-wired part of the mind that the program is required for survival and is reality. Your mind will start to operate from these facts and will start to make that programming true in your physical world.

Your mind doesn't understand fact from fiction, it only sees and believes what you program it to believe. Facts and fiction have equal footing in the mind, it doesn't understand the difference since it is not programmed to determine what is true or false, but rather accepts all soft-wire programming as true and required to continue surviving.

The mind can make fiction a fact and can make fact a fiction… depending on how you program it. To a child, Santa Claus delivering gifts is a fact and parents delivering gifts on Christmas night would be a fiction. Even if a child caught their parents putting gifts under the tree, they would assume that some other series of events were actually taking place, such as the gifts where already brought by Santa and the parents were just moving them around etc. Their minds will make their mental reality true without consideration of other possible truths. When children learn that Santa is not the person they thought, many continue to believe in Santa for a period of time. That is the power of successful mind programming.

Examples: If you have ever experienced losing weight suddenly, you will still see yourself through your mind's filter as heavier looking, at least for a while. If you had a radical hair-cut, your mind still sees your hair as it looked before the haircut.

[45]

CHAPTER 8

How to Program the Mind

Let's move this to a money-making situation to create a usable technique and example of how to use Mind Programming to create a new financial reality.

Since my background is in real estate, we'll use that for this example. But you can adapt this technique to any vehicle for gaining wealth or achieving any goal you desire.

To program the mind, you will use a technique in which you run a short mental video clip which is created and viewed only in your mind. It's like watching a "YouTube" video. It will last only a minute or so in duration. You will create the content of the clip based on what you desire. Then the actions to get there. You will play the same clips over and over in a pre-planned time frame.

I'll use a real estate transaction as an example to make this process easier to understand. To be successful in a real estate transaction, you must first see yourself being successful in a transaction, seeing it actually close and believe it has already happened.

The mental video clip will always involve some type of action on your part, and it must be seen as having already occurred. Add as much mental visualization of the event as possible, such as seeing yourself sign a contract with a seller, shaking hands with the seller, seeing a big smile on the seller's face and seeing yourself sign a contract with a happy buyer; and then walking into the title company and picking up a check.

You then complete the clip with the end results of depositing the money in your bank account and then feeling happy by spending some of the money on important desires which require money. You need to know the exact amount you earned from the deal to make it real to your mind. The greater the details experienced, the better the results.

After 5-days of running this mental video clip at least 4-times per day, replace the clip on the 6th day with just the first step needed to start the process rolling (the action step). That may be seeing yourself waking the next day and going to the computer where you start viewing home listings online. It can include seeing yourself picking up the phone and calling a seller to inquire about their home. It can include seeing a nice conversation between the two of you and ending with progress having been made. Now, run this clip a minimum 4 times and as many times as you can, throughout the 6th day.

Upon rising the 7th day, the mind will kick in and make that true. Continue running the "First Step" programming until you accomplish it. By continuing to run this program, you will be in a state of unrest until you complete the act. It will automatically send words to your brain that will allow a good and fruitful conversation to take place. It will create and unrest inside you until you accomplish the programming instilled in your mind.

Once you complete the first step, the tasks become much easier. The rest of the deal will seem to "just come together" as if by magic. Merlin the magician's magic was real. This is how we create something from nothing.

Once you have successfully closed your first transaction, do not replace your mental video clips with real events or real people. Keep the same video going but with added profit or added swiftness to closing.

The problem with replacing your success programming with real events is that it will also allow negative issues that occurred during real events to creep in as well. These small negative events that occur in all transactions will accumulate over time and cause you to become exhausted if allowed into your mind programming.

Let's look at just happened? Why did you have to complete a two-step mental video approach to affect your mind?

Let's examine it so you can then translate this to any task or desire you wish to make happen including becoming a millionaire. You will notice that we had more in our mental video than just the "end results" or the goal. We included the "means to the end" which is taking action. You may have seen motivational gurus instruct people to "just concentrate" on their goal and it will come. That simply isn't true. You can concentrate on whatever you want to attain and that won't make it happen. How many times have you day-dreamed about some event occurring which never ended up happening… even if you day-dreamed about it constantly? Why doesn't day-dreaming or focusing constantly on your goals make them come true if what these people teach is true?

The reason is that an overall "goal" or "desire" is not ACTION oriented. Seeing yourself with a million dollars in the bank and driving around in a limousine, or a gorgeous model on your arm is not an action event; those types of day-dreams or goals are "end results" only. Successful Mind Programming requires a means to an end, especially in the mental video clip.

End results are what we call the "HAVE" part of the cycle. We all want some end result such as becoming a millionaire, freedom to choose the life you want or other achievement. Achieving your goal is not a complete mind program. It is only one-third of the program. Goals and desires are the results of mind programming. You must also program the method of achieving the end results as well.

This is why "Millionaire Mind Programming" requires that you…

1. The goal, defined in detail. (the Have)

2. Establishing who you are (need to BE) in order to get it. Includes erasing NSP.
3. The first action step to set it all into motion (the Do) Includes writing down goals and actions as well as mind movies daily.

Programming for Millionaire Status

In programming yourself to become a millionaire, you will create a series of Mind Programs similar to those detailed in the last chapter. And when used successfully, will result in you first becoming a millionaire in your mind, then in your bank account. Let's begin by seeing what this will look like. While you can use any method you wish. You must start with an exact end result/goal you desire. You will first define what a millionaire means to you.

- **Is it someone with $1,000,000 in the bank?**
- **Is it someone earning $100,000 per month?**
- **Is it someone with $1,000,000.00 in equity in homes or assets?**
- **Is it someone with a credit line of $1,000,000?**
- **Or some other definition altogether, satisfying relationship, amazing career, great artist, etc.?**

Let's say your definition of a millionaire will be someone with $100,000 in monthly income from real estate deals.

Next, we will define the actions that will take place which will get us the goal as we detailed above. In real estate, this could translate into 4 closed home deals per month in which you earn at least $25,000 on each deal. Or it could be seen as 8 deals per month earning you $13,000 per month. In a network marketing business, this could translate into recruiting x number of people per day with a projected income from those recruits. You get the point.

You need to see exactly how the money would need to be created so you can see what your true number of closings need to be or the amount you see yourself earning in your mental video clips. Let's go with the first one in this example.

We now have our mental video clip content completed. These mental video clips are to be played over and over during the 6-week period. The next phase is to change the mental video clip content for the 6th week from "end results" to "first action steps" we defined in step 3 above.

To recap, you will take a few minutes, 4 times a day and play your mental video clip. Close your eyes and see the same clip running in your mind every day. You will see yourself finding customers. You see and hear customers agreeing with your presentations and offers. You see yourself closing the sale, cashing the check and spending the money on things you desire. YOU SEE ALL OF THIS AS HAVING ALREADY HAPPENED!

Play your "end results" program with its attached "means-to-the-end" over the 5-week period. In addition, study all available business training material, instructions, presentations, etc., as much as possible. In the final week, you will change the mental video from an "end results" type clip to one which contains the exact first steps you will need to take in order to start the process for your first deal. This clip could include scenes such as calling in ads, placing ads online, talking to customers, first phone contact with customers, and lining up your key documents. It will contain the first important steps to starting your business.

If you can run the program more than 4 times per day, then do so. Also, if you miss some sessions, don't worry about it, this is a 6-week process and missing a few will not affect your results. The key is keeping focused by repeating the process over and over again.

At the end of the 6th week, wake the following day and continue running the same mental video clip of the first step. Such as picking up the phone and calling someone, placing an ad, etc. Run the first step video clip until you physically complete the task.

As you have seen, a very important concept in achieving your goal or desire is to program your mind with action based mental video clips. This is called the BE phase of the Success Cycle. You are preparing your mind for what to DO and BE.

[53]

CHAPTER 9

Preventing Failure

Have you ever started a job or a business that seemed great and exciting, but over time, it became a major chore or pain to do? Well, you experienced exhaustion with that event. Exhaustion is caused by boredom, lack of challenge, or an accumulation of small negative occurrences over time.

Exhaustion is the number one reason why people stop being successful once success is attained.

This same phenomenon will occur in anything you do if you don't know how to address the issue. This includes making $10,000 or even $100,000 a month. At some point it seems like it becomes difficult or a major pain to continue doing.

We can prevent exhaustion from occurring by creating challenges to an otherwise boring sequence of events; and by viewing the small negative occurrences as welcome challenges to be solved along the way. Make it into a game. Part of soft-wiring your Mind is to become a problem solver as well as a millionaire. This will prevent exhaustion from occurring.

The easiest way to create challenges is to constantly raise the bar on how fast and how much you can achieve. Which seems to be the exact opposite of what you would think you should do. But it works.

You can also add additional things you do with the money you make, such as in helping a good cause etc.

When you are ready for success, then you will find all the tools and methods needed to become successful. There's an old saying… "When the student is ready, the teacher will appear." The same can be said for the vehicle to wealth. The vehicle is the actual business that you use to become a millionaire. When the student is ready, the vehicle to wealth will appear.

[57]

CHAPTER 10

3 KEYS TO SUCCESS

The 1st Key to success is realizing that you must BE, before you can HAVE.

To be successful, you must first program your mind for success. It must believe that success already is your reality. Use the mind programming techniques in this book to achieve this step.

The 2nd Key to success is to be willing to RISK and lose, and accept that you can come back from the possible loss.

To risk, you must have something on the line that you would feel as a loss. This is usually money, which is typically the investment you make in your business.

There is no greater motivation than FEAR OF LOSS. When you decide on the risk you will take, you will not want to incur any loss. Rather than not taking the risk, what you should be focusing on, to do everything possible to succeed and not let anything get in your way to success. The more you risk, the harder you will work not to lose your investment. Only a fool tries to start a business with no investment or risk.

The 3rd Key to success is that you must not stop on the path to success once you start.

When you run into a brick wall… which you will; you must continue looking for ways to get around, over, under, or through the wall. Controlling the beginning and the continuation of your system should be your only concern when striving for success.

In order to not stop, you must be willing to put in the WORK. It will be hard work, nothing simple comes to you with the right mindset. Mindset allows you to succeed at the work you will now put into your business. Mindset allows you to not self-sabotage your work. Mindset allows your work to bring 10-times the results without it. Mindset allows optimum work performance. Mindset provides the trajectory and work provides the thrust for your hard work. The hard work is the "DO" part of the equation.

CHAPTER 11

It Happens in Three's

Whenever we succeed or fail at something, it was because we followed a 3-step process, whether we knew it or not. I call these 3 steps process a Success Cycle. There are actually three processes at work in any success cycle. Each cycle begins by "starting" something, then "moving it forward", and at some point, "stopping" the process. The two hardest to accomplish parts of any cycle are starting it and moving it forward; while the easiest is stopping it or quitting. And for everything there is the right time to stop it or change it.

Among a few other things we will cover later which prevent starting or moving it forward, are procrastination and fear. Fear and negative thoughts can also stop the cycle.

Charles Haanel first published the idea of the BE, DO, and HAVE Theory in 1912. Countless authors and business instructors have since used this idea in their material. I'll be expanding on his work in this book.

CHAPTER 12

The Success Cycle

There are 3 phases to a success cycle. BE, DO, and HAVE. You must first BE that which you desire, in order to DO what actions are required in order to HAVE your end results. Most people run this out of order and is why 95% of the population struggles financially.

Most people DO in order to BE, so they can HAVE. For example, they will do any job to be "employed" so they can pay bills. People (DO) what is already programmed in their mind (BE) and hope they get their wish (HAVE). People who see success as "being employed" have a program running that says, they are limited to being employed as the only means for making money. They are an "employee", period.

Two gentlemen from the same small city in Louisiana attended one of my seminars together. They sat next to each other in the room. They each heard the same teachings, each understood what was taught, and each walked out saying they knew they could "do it."

One year later, one of the gentlemen, Don S. came back to take another seminar on a different topic. Don explained that he had earned over 1.6 million dollars since taking the first seminar. I asked about his friend and he said that he had never even started a single deal. He said after the seminar, the man just went back to work at his old job.

Here was a person who received everything Don had received in the way of training and still failed. This other man simply wasn't ready for success. His mind stopped him from an obviously easy trip to millionaire status. This man remained at his old job because his programming told him he was an "employee" not a "millionaire." Many business owners, still possess this "employee" mindset.

Let's jump into the BE/DO/HAVE cycle at a deeper level to see why it is so powerful. This is one of the most important components in achieving the right mind set.

BE DO HAVE

The BE, DO, and HAVE Cycle is occurring in your life right now on many different levels and in many different areas of your life.

1. Everyone is always at some point in the BE, DO, HAVE cycle in multiple aspects of their life.
2. One may stop the cycle at any time and change the BE or DO in order to change the HAVE.
3. Only the BE and DO are the variable stages we need to address in order to HAVE.
4. The Universe must react to our BE and DO states and provide us our HAVE. If you don't see the HAVE, it's because of something wrong in the Be or Do area.
5. The BE must be re-programmed before the DO can be changed.

Since you are reading this type of book, you are most likely seeking a new HAVE. You are looking for a change. All changes start with the BE, DO, HAVE cycle. This requires that you now change the order of your thoughts so that a new direction can be achieved by a new set of Beliefs.

In further understanding of the principles that make up the BE, DO, HAVE cycle, we find a mathematical equation at work… BE + DO = HAVE.

An exact BE combined with the exact DO will always result in a preconceived HAVE condition. This is also why following a good method to achieve a goal works well when the BE and DO are addressed from the beginning. For example, a franchise or business system is the DO part of an equation. If you add the right BE, then we know what HAVE will result. Here is what a mind program might look like for a McDoogles's franchise owner. *"I'm a successful McDoogles franchise owner because I'm doing what other successful McDoogles franchise owners do."* It's easy for franchise owners to see themselves as successful owners. And this program will go far in making it so.

Even though there may have been many McDoogle franchise owners fail; this is never focused on by the Company or the Franchisee.

Most existing franchise or business systems have a proven track record that speaks for itself. If a person has the right frame of mind and uses a good business system correctly, they succeed, if they have the wrong frame of mind or wrong DO process, they will fail.

Franchises help make the BE condition easier to adapt to because a person automatically thinks they will BE a successful franchise owner because others have been successful doing the same thing. They actually see themselves as a successful owner before they even start to run the business. The same effect happens when a person enters a coaching program or a mastermind.

The BE, DO, HAVE is in perfect alignment with most franchises/coaching programs or ready to use business systems. People who startup businesses from scratch don't have the history to support a success mentality. They often fear the business will fail for a number of reasons. This is why it is very difficult to create a new type of business that becomes successful. The "success" BE is missing by default.

If you didn't discover the BE, DO, HAVE Theory, you might have continued to just hope or wish for a different HAVE condition. You might have started back on the same BE, DO phase which results in your previous HAVE condition. You are now armed with something very powerful.

People who have not prepared the BE condition correctly often explain, "Nothing ever changes in my life." This is because they continue in their existing BE condition. They wish for a different HAVE condition but are running an existing BE Mind Program. If your BE programming makes you an "employee", then you can wish for whatever you want but only "employee" HAVE's will keep occurring.

Most people make the mistake of just changing the DO and wishing for the HAVE and neglecting the BE altogether. Just wishing, praying, or hoping for a new end result. They have by-passed the BE part, making it impossible to achieve the new HAVE.

The proper course of action is to decide what outcome you desire (HAVE). Then firmly see yourself with these results (BE) as already accomplished; along with a course of action (DO) to make it occur. Speak and think about it as if it were already done. The (HAVE) can now occur. You can now see why we incorporate this concept into our mental videos.

CHAPTER 13

How to Begin any Success Cycle

Now that we know how to use the BE, DO, HAVE Theory, let's now look at how to use the cycle to determine what it is we need to BE in order to DO in order to HAVE. It must always start with the HAVE condition.

Before any goal is conceived, start by determining what end results you desire. Do you want to travel to the moon? Then you must BE an astronaut in your mind long before you become an astronaut in the physical world.

Becoming a Millionaire means discovering the vehicle, the business plan, others have used to become millionaires. It also means deciding on the BE that fits you best.

As an example, being a "Soldier of Fortune" could get you to a millionaire status, but not without a lot of danger and risk of losing your life. Determine what makes you feel happy, what challenges your mind, and what keeps you interested.

Find someone who has already made a million in your preferred business and start there. Ask yourself if you are passionate about that field, and could you see yourself being like that person who made it to the top.

As a child, did anyone ever ask you what you wanted to be when you grew up? Or what you wanted to do when you graduated school? These are both BE and DO phases having been pushed on you before you understood what you wanted to have and what kind of life you wanted to live, the HAVING part of life.

Without first knowing what you wish to have, it would be hard to decide what to be or do. This is why so many college students switch degrees or just drop out of college altogether. They never asked themselves what results they wanted before deciding what to become.

Which would be a clearer view to a young person seeking a career? Be on call 24-hours a day for the rest of your career, which also creates an 80% chance of divorce. Fill out Government paperwork 70% of your work time. Enough of your customers will sue you to drain most of your profits for the first half of your career. One wrong decision could cause you to lose your career and have to start over again. Endure all this after 10 years of daily study to become a Medical Doctor.

Being a Doctor means HAVING the things a Doctor has and must deal with. The having part is not written up in the College handbooks, just the picture of being a Doctor looking at an X-ray next to a shapely nurse. No wonder so many Doctors become disenchanted with the profession before long. No wonder you may have found yourself in a go no-where job doing something you don't really want to do. No wonder you may not be earning the kind of money you want.

The HAVING conditions you are now in, may not have been part of your original game plan when you were looking at Being what you are today.

The good news is that you can change it with what you are learning here, it's never too late! A while back, an attendee at one of my seminars was an 85-year-old man. He came up to me after the seminar was over and said, "I just wished I had learned all this 5 years ago." So, unless you are over 80, you now know for sure it's not too late for you to implement massive changes in your life.

SPECIALIZED KNOWLEDGE

One of the requirements of starting a profitable Success Cycle is implementing or capitalizing on some type of specialized knowledge. In the book, "Think and Grow Rich" by Napoleon Hill, you will find one of the key concepts Hill discovered is that all wealthy people use SPECIALIZED KNOWLEDGE.

In fact, there is a whole chapter on this one concept in Hill's book. Hill explains that specialized knowledge is not the same thing as "general knowledge" which you learn at a college or school; rather, it is something more exact.

Let's expand on Napoleon Hill's definition of specialized knowledge. Specialized knowledge is information that provides a process which instructs you in the exact step-by-step procedure in accomplishing something. But it can also be a formula/system for doing form or part of a business. This could be a coaching program, a mentoring program, or a procedure for accomplishing something unique. I like to use Bill Gates as an example of this; Bill Gates bought the rights to DOS (the main coding needed to run Windows) for next to nothing, and then turned it into the biggest enterprise in world history. DOS is also a "Specialized Knowledge." Controlling that knowledge made its owners very rich. Running any kind of system that has proven to work is also a type of specialized knowledge.

But specialized knowledge has one other important partner required to make specialized knowledge the "right" knowledge that helps one the most. That other piece is TIMING, also known as OPPORTUNITY.

Acting on or using specialized knowledge at the right time is very important. IBM had one and only one opportunity to purchase the DOS operating system and Windows technology before Bill Gates decided to create the Window's Company himself. Gates first offered it to IBM. IBM heard him out and made a colossal mistake by passing on it. As a result, IBM lost the top position it had attained in the technology business arena with that missed opportunity.

The window of opportunity opens and shuts without asking anyone's permission. Most people don't see or notice the was even open until after the window has shut and the opportunity gone forever.

A smart business person must see both the specialized knowledge component and the window of opportunity as well. When both these components meet great fortunes are made by those that act quickly. Great opportunities happen every day and in every market.

In the current market, there is tremendous opportunity as more and more people need solutions to problems they have never faced before. Specialized knowledge you gain from a company like mine, or other companies that focus on meeting the needs of people in the current marketplace (timing) will give you the greatest profits you may see for years to come. The great part is that you get to help people while making money.

There are great opportunities in the network marketing field as well. During economic downturns, people seek extra income and these companies historically do especially well during recessions or high unemployment. Finding a company whose products and services cater to the needs of today's mass market is important when choosing one. I've been involved with several over the years and continue even today with one that complements my existing business.

At one time, I ran the same poor programming many people do in regards to network marketing companies until I started meeting people in my seminars who had done quite well with them. Some even made over a million a year. That poor mind programming was quick to go!

Whether you are using business plan, network marketing, a coaching program, the latest marketing systems, or some other vehicle to attain your wealth and financial security, remember that unlike what Hill taught, specialized knowledge must be paired correctly with timing in order to work.

To create massive income, watch for the open window and take action when specialized knowledge and opportunity come together.

CHAPTER 14

Affirmation Programming

Affirmations are a form of mini self-talk programming session that can have a dramatic effect on those that use the technique. An affirmation can be as simple as repeating "I am a millionaire" over and over during the day. I constantly use this affirmation to maintain what I have built.

I use affirmations to keep myself focused and complete tasks that need to be completed. I also use affirmations to give myself instructions and commands. You can get so much more done during the day by verbally instructing yourself to do something within a certain timeframe.

When you are your own boss, there is no outside boss to guide you in completing tasks, keeping priorities or breaking bad work habits. You can use simple quick commands to help yourself during the day. "I will get the paperwork completed in the next 2 hours"; "I will not answer emails before 11:00 am." A next level and far more effective affirmation is using the same statements in past tense. "I got the paperwork competed"; "I never answer emails before 11:00am."

Affirmations can be used for both short term and long-term effects. An affirmation is a cause of effects in your life. What do you want to have happen in your life? Use every cause you can to create it. Affirmations will be one of the components to attaining your HAVE effects.

Millionaire Affirmations

- I am a millionaire! I will seek out and find other people to help become millionaires. Nothing will stop me from finding other people to help become millionaires, so that I may continue living the millionaire's life.

- I do what millionaires do.

- It's OK to do what millionaires do.

- And yet, I remain a millionaire
- As a millionaire, I will see a return on my invested money.

- I am earning more and more money every day.

- I will encourage anyone I speak with to become wealthy by taking action now.

- People I talk with can always raise money if they want to.

- Everyone wants to earn money, no matter what they say.

- Everyone needs money and I can help them get it.

- I speak as a millionaire speaks.

- I think as a millionaire thinks.

- I act as a millionaire acts.

- I avoid negative people and seek positive people

- Nothing is impossible or too big for me to accomplish.

- I respect other people's opinions, but it's my opinion in the end, that I act on.

- I have released my inner millionaire which has changed my life financially.

- As a millionaire, I leverage as much as I can in every deal.

- I remain a millionaire because I excel at accomplishing all my daily tasks.

- I am the best in the world at what I do. That's how I remain a millionaire

- I'm not shy about blowing my own horn since no one else will blow it for me.

- As a millionaire, I love speaking in front of people.

- As a millionaire, I take charge in all business dealings.

- As a millionaire, I love sales, I'm great at sales.

- As a millionaire, I always take responsibility, it's up to me to make changes and get things completed.

- I attract other millionaires and people who want to become millionaires.

Using Affirmations to Reprogram Negative Survival Programs (NSP)

Affirmations are also the best way to remove survival programs. The cause of most problems stem from the inability to start, inability to continue forward, or inability to stop something in your life. When you face a problem, its eventual outcome will be determined by one or more NSPs which need to be discovered, documented and reversed.

Besides saying Affirmations, you must also WRITE THEM DOWN. Write them down in a notebook once a day at a minimum, twice a day if possible. Nothing hardwires the brain faster than writing down affirmations. While you are writing down affirmations, you also want to write down your daily and end goals (results). This keeps you focused on getting the actions completed each day. The act of writing is a stronger way to the mind. It imprints on the mind when you write, see and hear yourself.

When you feel you have hit a wall or something outside of you is stopping you from progressing; it may well be NSP that is causing the real problem. It is usually your current NSP that will mix false beliefs with past experiences/facts and bring you to a complete stop.

NSPs are easy to spot once you examine the issue causing the problem. Your mind takes known facts or past experiences and adds one or more false beliefs usually based on preconceived fears; then delivers you your current condition. By dissecting the issue, you are able to assign each component of a NSP to fact or fiction. This can now be attacked directly by new programming via the use of the following affirmation structure.

Create the structure by writing down these impressions. First write down the issue stopping or preventing you from going forward. Next, write down your first major impression of how you feel about the issue. Then write down how you feel from a past, present, and future perspective about the issue stopping you. You may also find that you have more than one NSP that will need to be addressed in the same manner.

For example, let us say you are trying to make your business profitable but are about to give up because you find yourself saying "I've tried everything to make my business profitable and nothing is going to work... so I'm ready to quit and do something else."

The facts are that you may have tried many things. The false belief is that you have tried everything. To feel you have tried everything means the mind will not try anything else since it believes you have tried everything. If you are verbalizing or just thinking you have tried everything your mind starts to shut down other avenues of possible changes that could be made to make your business profitable.

The next part of your belief says "nothing is going to work." Is this a fact or a false belief? You can now see how to dissect any issue (belief) that you feel is stopping your progress. It's always best to write out your feelings about the issue on paper and look at each component of the statement. Ask yourself if this is a fact or just a false belief.

Once you have separated fact from fiction, you will then compile your affirmation designed to reverse the effects of the negative survival program. You can use the following simple affirmation designed to address and fix most issues. The wording will be the same for almost any issue you face. It uses two assumptions which you can easily believe.

Assumptions:
1. **Somebody else has experienced your current issue (or something close enough) and has overcome it.**

2. **If somebody else can do something, so can you.**

This is the affirmation example using these assumptions… "Other people have (fill in the blank with your issue) and have (fill in the blank to overcome it). Whatever someone else can do, I can do."
Example: "Other people have had businesses that were not successful and have made them profitable. Whatever somebody else can do, I can do."

The Trilogy of Affirmations

In the final step, you now create a statement that creates a past successful event out of your issue. This is the second part of your affirmation. In this case, it would look something like this.

"My business is very profitable now and I have additional ideas to make it even more profitable."

Your completed affirmation will look like this.
"Other people have had businesses that were not successful and have made them profitable. Whatever somebody else can do, I can do. My business is very profitable now and I have additional ideas to make it even more profitable."

Repeat this affirmation several times a day for several days, then at least once a day until you can see the changes taking place in your life.

Next, use the magic wand, some call a pen to write out this affirmation on the enchanted scroll; known today as a piece of paper. This action, seals this into your unconscious faster than just saying it. It's taking words and which are normally visual and auditory into tactile format. This is the third leg of the method. The Trilogy of Affirmations… Mind/Body/Spirit, Be/Do/Have, See/Hear/Touch.

And finally, examine other possible survival programs you are running that could be creating the issue you face. You are likely to have more than just one false belief that is contributing to the main issue. Dissect each one the same way and reprogram them as well.

CHAPTER 15

On Cause and Effect

A millionaire is a Cause; a poor person is an Effect. More correctly, maintaining millionaire status is a Cause. Remaining a poor person is an Effect. You will always make things happen or let things happen in your life.

When you make things happen, you are a Cause. When you let things happen, you are an Effect.

This means programs running inside your mind are the causes of your current condition. But more importantly, they will be the cause of your future condition, which can be changed.

By not taking action, you become an Effect. Whenever you take action, you are living your life as the Cause. The greater number of actions you create, the more likely you will get what you want in life. To gain more in life, take action at every opportunity. Don't watch, act! You will still have negative conditions happening in your life when your actions don't work out, but you will feel you have control over your life. As long as you feel you have control, you can create more actions that can bring the changes to get you what you want in life.

11 Causes of Success in Business

BE

1. Write down your goals in exact detail of what it will take along with a time frame to achieve them; review it often.

2. Talk to yourself in a positive way. Build yourself up, from your mind up. Tell yourself you already have it. See yourself as already having it. Act like what you want to be. It took 15 billion years for the Universe to create you exactly as you are now. That can't be a mistake. That's perfection; you are a perfect creation of the Universe. Now what are you going to do with that historic effort?

3. Get properly prepared. Shortcut your way to success by relying on history and those that came before you. Very few things are new; success is a proven road travelled by others before you. Find them and get their assistance on your road to success.

4. Learn just enough to start a project, don't worry about the middle or finish, you can always learn and adjust as you go along. You can't succeed if you don't start something in a fairly quick manner. Act now!

5. Learn from past mistakes by building from them, not dwelling on them. Mistakes and failures are required to be made by those that succeed. You will need to get comfortable with this fact in order to succeed.

6. Sound confident, even when you aren't. To Be Confident, Act Confident.

DO

7. Do it NOW! Putting it off creates an 80% chance it won't ever get done.

8. Plan your work and work your plan. Plan your day out each morning. Write down important items to be completed, and hold yourself accountable for not working the plan. Put in the hard work required.

9. Listen to opinions of others, but realize they are just that, opinions. No one cares as much about your business as you. Make sure the people you listen to have the same kind of bank balance you desire.

10. Never stop going forward. Let nothing get in your way. If you can't move it out of the way, change your angle, but don't stop the forward momentum. Starting and Good Momentum is 90% of success.

11. Worry won't help any situation and will in fact, draw to you what you fear. Fear is conquered by confronting it. Facing your fears with the support of others will make it easier. Find like individuals facing the same fear and share success stories and encouragement.

HAVE Results: Success

Causes of Failure in Business are the opposite causes of success. When failure happens, it can often be attributed to one of these causes.

BE
1. Unclear Goals and Time Frames
2. Negative Self-Talk
3. Lack of Preparation
4. Over-Analysis
5. Thoughts of Past Failures
6. Lack of Confidence

DO
7. Procrastination
8. No Daily Plan of Action, no work
9. Influenced from negative outsiders/authority figures. Believe the news.
10. Lack of Persistence
11. Worry and Fear of possible Negative Effects

HAVE Results: Failure

CHAPTER 16

25 Secrets That Will Explode Your Business

Most of this book centered on how to start BEING a millionaire. Now let's look at some DO parts of being a millionaire. Besides finding the vehicle (the business) that will take you to millionaire status, I have found many DO parts that have been useful with any vehicle you decide to use, especially if they involve running a home-based business.

My 30-plus years of running my own home-based business; has taught me some valuable rules to follow. While I could have easily gone into the corporate world, even to the point of almost taking my own company public, HAVING certain things was not worth giving up the pleasures of working from home. My BE would have completely changed, it would have killed my HAVE (home based business I run in just a few hours a day.)

I and many of my clients continue to achieve income levels that only CEO's of public corporations earn and with none of the stress. That's my definition of success and happiness. Yours may be different. However, I will include the rules and resources I use for running one of the most successful home-based businesses in the country.

In a home-based business, almost none of following business concepts ever change and can be used by anyone in a home-based business.

1. Invest as little as possible in business setup expenses when starting a business, however, ensure you are committed to spending the required amount of money to get you COMMITTED and ensure success. There should always be a financial commitment of some amount on your part when starting any business. It should be enough to make you feel uncomfortable but not worried you would lose your shirt if it doesn't work out.

2. You must be HELPING your customers in order to earn the maximum profits, the bigger their problem, the bigger your profit.

3. Deal only in the LARGER TICKET ITEMS. It takes the same amount of time and effort to sell a $100.00 item as it does to sell a $10,000.00 to $100,000 item, and often less time and with less problems. The profit is bigger on the larger priced item. You can sell less, advertise

less than you would need to for the smaller item. You have less complaints and problems with fewer customers paying larger amounts as well.

4. You should always DISCLOSE as much as possible to other parties as long as you are not revealing trade secrets or information that could be used against you by bad faith acts on the part of others. Maintain maximum communication with your current customers.

5. Always look for NEW PROBLEMS that your customer faces and find ways to overcome them. This is the key to staying in business long term and making the largest profits in any business. New products should always act to "solve" your customer's problems.

6. Stand up for your rights and let no one steal your rights or dreams. The world will take what you won't defend, and its favorite items to steal are your legal rights, your business, and your dreams. Keep good records.

7. The world gives you just enough to survive; you must earn the rest yourself. Charity and Government Assistance is a trap which holds you back. It creates an unwritten contract that binds you to the Giver. Unless you have children that are going hungry, avoid it at all costs.

8. Don't be afraid to talk about your accomplishments because no one else is going to blow your horn for you.

9. Develop a MASTERMIND GROUP or find a mentor as soon as possible. Ask for help from them when you can't solve a business problem. Make sure the advice you take is coming from someone that is highly successful in the profession connected to the business you are pursuing. I have seen so many investors make the mistake of taking investing advice from real estate agents or business advice from attorneys. Most agents are not investors and most lawyers don't run great businesses. Ask agents how to fill out contracts, and ask lawyers about legal questions within their certification. Ask a great investor about investing. Ask a successful business owner your business questions.

10. Keep a MARKETING PLAN going that puts you in communication with at least 15 new people every day. Use websites, email, and direct phone conversations for communication with customers.

11. Belly-to-Belly communication is the best way to build early in your business, then move to phone communication as your business grows, then to web-based communication as you explode your growth.

12. Don't be quick to believe the media when it reports business news, all press releases have profit motives behind them. But don't totally disregard them either.

13. Learn how to speak in public and hold public presentations as soon as possible.

14. Master attracting customers, fulfilling services/products to those customers, and retaining

those customers as life-time customers, as soon as possible. The future of all business will revolve around these key components.

15. Learn about the latest website systems if you are able or at least have a source that can create them for you. Most customers want a system that has the least amount of friction to using it. Make it easy for your client to do business with you. Your competition is often the best source for finding the latest means of internet marketing resources.

16. Don't work in General Partnerships if at all possible. Use Joint Ventures designed for short periods as a replacement when funds are low and you must form a partnership to go forward. Partnerships are like marriage while joint ventures are like dating. Joint ventures give you more freedom in your business future. A joint venture allows you to partner with just a limited scope of operation while a general partnership forces you into splitting profits across a wide range of businesses.

17. Would you like to make your business grow ten times faster than it is right now? On one of your days off, write down the goals you need to accomplish during the upcoming week. The type of goal you list must be able to be completed during the week. Putting it in writing is the key to getting it done. You will feel a commitment not otherwise felt to complete the tasks. I eventually created a Book that does just this for you. It's called **"The Millionaire Day Planner"**. Buy it on Amazon. Fill out your goals and even the problem

issues daily. You will see improvements in your business in just days by using it.

18. If a customer turns you down, always leave them something that can help them in their aims and ask nothing in return for this help.

19. Customers that elect not to do business with you now, should continue to be contacted on a regular basis. These customers will buy when they are ready, not necessarily when you are ready.

20. Starting a new business will always require a certain amount of faith; evidence and past results can't be counted on.

21. Maximize your leverage in all business dealings. Controlling a lot, with a little; is what leverage is all about. An Option Agreement allows you the maximum return for your investment in real estate and can be adapted to other businesses as well. A partnership is a form of leverage. Having specialized knowledge is a form of leverage as well.

22. Develop MULTIPLE PROFIT CENTERS that compliments your main business. The best centers will be affiliate or networking programs. Affiliate programs tend to pay smaller amounts, but they can add up. You should always market additional products and services to your customer base. People like buying from companies and people with whom they are already trust and doing business. Find complimentary products and services to maximize your sales. But go

Vertical, not Horizontal when it comes to adding businesses or other forms of income to your existing one.

23. Avoid investing in Stocks, Bonds, Commodities, Options, Currency and anything else that has to do with Wall Street. Invest first in growing your business. You will invest in your business on an on-going basis. You should never stop putting profits back into growing your business by expanding your advertising budget, then by improving your business. Next, invest in your own home; and when you earn more money, invest in a bigger home. Pay all extra money toward paying off your home and keep your debts as low as possible. Debt is only good if used correctly and kept in balance with your cash-flow.

24. Buy assets, not liabilities. Most cars are a liability since they depreciate quicker than most people can pay it off. You want to buy things that go up in value over time, not down. There are some cars and classic cars that go up or at least retain their value. You will always either "spend" your money, or "invest" your money. Millionaires invest! Coaching and Courses are investments, business software is an investment, masterminding and learning specialized knowledge is an investment.

25. Don't sell your products, services, or time too cheaply. Lower prices mean you have to sell more in order to turn a profit. When you start to think you should lower your prices, always raise your prices instead and add more value to justify the increase. You

will do better by raising prices whenever you feel that you should lower your prices. Perceived value and higher profit margins are better ways of turning a profit than lowering revenue and increasing sales costs and lowering perceived value. Only mega large companies have the luxury of lowering prices and still turning a good profit.

Don't sell to the person who is not yet climbing the ladder of success. That's the group of people that complain the most and can never be satisfied. They have the worst mind programs running that make it impossible to be happy, much less appreciative. They need someone else who can serve them better than what you can. Instead, offer to help the person who is climbing the ladder of success already, the higher you can aim on the ladder, the better. One of your prominent sales messages should be aimed at the very top of that ladder. But also, know your ladder. Who is your ideal client? Where did they start climbing the ladder and where do they usually get to on the ladder before needing help. Next, ask what parts of that ladder needs you or your product/service to help be the bridge for your client. Learn how to just be the rung that your ideal client needs to allow them to continue climbing. Be the rung, is how you can serve your clients the most?

Always be Changing

Mother Nature starts fires to clear forests and when it's time, so should you. I have ended more businesses or business systems within a business than I can remember. You will have to improve as well as replace portions of your businesses to keep it growing. Replace and improve are two different things. You want to improve a process that is working but could be better, but you end and often replace a process that has failed. Those who can't embrace change will not make it in business. If something isn't changing, it's dying or already dead.

Chapter 17

The Key to Helping Your Client Achieve All their Dreams

Your client already knows how to accomplish their goals, they just don't implement what they know in order to make achieve them.

Your number one job is to use the strategies in this book to tap into their mind and adjust it where and when needed to keep them going in the right direction.

Think of it this way; they are an Uber Driver and you are the passenger and their phone stopped working. They know how to drive the car, how to navigate traffic, etc.

What they need now is direction. And if they follow these directions, they will reach their destination.

Get clarity on your client's goals. Then look at what is preventing them from achieving them. To do this, you will need to examine your client's Negative Survival Programming in addition to the actual physical business-based limitations such as a lack of quality marketing systems, customer retention, and other systems you know how to help them with.

As said above, these are minor issues that are easy fixes to most business. It's the mental issues that prevent the client from implementing them that is the most common issue.

CHAPTER 18

Leverage Your Way Up

Do you know that over 80% of all millionaires are self-made? They didn't get their money from mom and dad or an inheritance. They actually had to go out and earn it themselves.

They learned it the hard way most of time. Some people were smarter and joined in with mentors and mastermind groups that helped them speed up the process.

I finally realized that there were some people that were a lot smarter than I was in the business world and I would learn from them every chance I could.

In every business I run, I put together a group of like-minded individuals and we helped each other along the road to our mutual success.

Every major financial leap in your life will occur because you were able to connect in some personal way with somebody much further along than yourself. These mentors will share their insight and information with you so you can get a free pass over all the hard spots and all the walls that the normal person has to climb over to become wealthy.

How do you get a big boost financially for the future? **Simply leverage somebody else's knowledge.** Use knowledge and wisdom of your mentor and boost yourself that much further and that much quicker along the path to financial freedom. Every great thing that I created or advanced in my business came directly from interacting with an individual or individuals that helped me connect with **that** which made it possible.

This is the power of a Mastermind Group or a great mentor. They send you on a warp-speed journey to financial wealth and prosperity.

We have talked a lot about what to do and little about what not to do. What to avoid doing can be as important as what to do. One of the biggest challenges for anyone going into business is FEAR. Most people focus on it, which means they are mind programming fear into their Being.

I was recently talking with a new client; in the conversation she explained all the things that could go wrong. She explained how a number of things could go wrong. And before she knew it, she had a whole list of things that she could pretty well count on going wrong. She really just wanted me to make her feel better by reassuring her that they would not go wrong. The problem was that I couldn't tell her nothing would go wrong. I instructed her not to focus on things that may not go right. And hearing that most likely made her even more afraid. That's because she is letting others control her future by trying to get guarantees where none exists. There is a difference between expecting things to go wrong and preparing for things should they go wrong. Expecting things to go wrong will program failure.

You can see right away where her mind was focused. It was actually looking for a way to FAIL. It is a very common survival program that people have running without realizing it.

Conversely, the correctly programmed mind, questions in a different manner. They say, "Well, what if I do this? Will that work? And will this make it better? And if I do that, can I make more money that way?" I'm not saying NOT to prepare for things going wrong, all you should do is realize they may, but certainly don't start expecting them to go wrong.

Unfortunately, people will set themselves up to failing by focusing on the negative, on the things that could go wrong. By doing this, they bring on the very things their minds are making true and real. Fear can paralyze you and prevent you from taking action which then leads to failure.

Think of fear as a disease, it is contagious just like a sickness. It is spread by and between people when they come in contact with each other. Like any sickness, it is better to have been inoculated from it and never have to deal with curing it once you catch it.

Like a virus, fear can pass from one person to the next with just one exposure in a short amount of time.

Next time you do something that was based on someone else's fear or when you see or hear fear in another's words; remember this key in dealing with their sickness. It is a sickness that only they suffer from. It was most likely passed to them from another. But it does not have to pass to you. Just see it when you hear it and that can go a long way toward preventing its deadly spread.

Fear can also sound like a warning. It comes in the form of over-caution or over-analysis, not taking risks, procrastination, accepting other people's past bad experiences. The problem is that bad experiences don't come with the other side of the story. Fear keeps 95% of the population working for corporations at a month-to-month survival wage while waiting for a retirement.

The U.S. Government Accountability Office (GAO) says that the average retirement fund for an American is $40,000 at age 62-65. Add that to the $400 monthly social security check and how and where will most live? They will have no choice but to continue working at low wages just to eat and pay for shelter. They have been lied to and are scared into giving up hope for true financial security.

The government is also hard at work, supporting the corporate giants. Job security is like living in the Matrix. Most people keep taking the colored pill and follow along with 95% of the population who believe and do what they are told… until they finally wake up at age 65 and it's too late to do anything about it. Then they keep your mouth shut because they are ashamed of having been suckered into the lie. There has never been real "job security" in this country, unless you owned the business.

Here's another fear I wanted to include because I hear it constantly. Customers will say, "That technique won't work in my city, we're too large" And then in another conversation, I might hear somebody say "That's not going to work in my town because we are too small." And then from another, "I live in the suburbs it can't possibly work here."

People who fail always seemed to have an excuse. Excuses are a justification of why they should fail. When you think about this, all these different people from all these different areas are saying "it won't work where I live" and yet at the same time there are successful people in all these same areas.

Learn to see poor mind programming in others as well as yourself so you can guard against it. True failures will play the "Blame Game." They feel they failed at something because of someone else. They refuse to look at their own contribution to their failure. By not allowing themselves to be at fault ensures their NSPs will continue to keep them in their pity party and failed condition.

CHAPTER 19

Putting it all Together

Let's summarize the ideas we have covered so you can see how the overall game-plan should come together.

Find a field you are passionate about where others have become a millionaire. Ensure the product or services are needed in the current marketplace. Learn the business as much as possible as quickly as possible. Don't expect to become an expert, that won't happen for another 20 years. Just get the basics down and start. Use the mind programming method detailed in this book. To help program yourself to be a millionaire, start using self-talk and affirmations on a daily basis. Join or create a mastermind group or locate a mentor as soon as possible.

Invest in yourself every week by learning new information about your business. Learn as much specialized knowledge as possible in your field through other individuals who have already cleared the way. Obtain on-going education and constant updates as markets change. You are to attain and remain at the top of the food chain in your industry.

Final Thoughts

Understand that we all hit brick walls, but also understanding that a wall has so many ways that can be surmounted. I share this story all the time in my seminars and webinars, "A wall can be climbed over, gone around to the left or to the right. You can dig a tunnel underneath it or you can take a stick of dynamite and blow it up." Until you have tried at least 5 ways to surmount a problem, don't give up. Most people give up after 1 or two attempts.

Success requires that you be decisive and ACT NOW. It requires that you make decisions and stick to it once you do.

There are multiple ways to get through the wall. Understand that walls will be there. But when you have the knowledge and the understanding, you can handle the walls. Everything else is simply mental. You can let the walls keep you back by focusing on the wall and saying, "I can't get past this wall." or "What if there are more walls?"

Or you can say, "There will be walls and there will be ways to get around each of them. I have already gotten past them."

Make it a point to read this book again every 3 months on your path to millionaire. It will help keep you motivated and focused along the way. As you can go back over this material and read this over and over again, important points will sink in and take root. It will make such a difference in your life that you will absolutely be astonished with the results.

Is This Your Defining Moment?

You may be at your defining moment in your life right now. You may realize you are going in the wrong direction and that you must change something in order to change your future. You will know it when you are presented with the right information. You know that you will need to drop some things in life and pick up other things in order to get on the right path. You will need to invest in yourself, invest in your family, and invest in your future.

Take the techniques and information found in this book and use them to redirect and reprogram your mind and your life. Leverage your way up to success. Only great things are in store for your life if you do. If you don't, you could miss out on the life you were supposed to have.

I look forward to hearing about your programmed success.
...John Alexander

[109]

Books by John Alexander

Writing Down Your Daily Goals is Key

How to Flip Vacant Lots
Available at

https:SelfFundingFlip.com

Living Trusts for Real Estate Investors

Stop Exposing Your Name and Assets to Lawsuits and Competition

Corporate entities have their place as liability protection, but they don't protect all the other properties the company may own, and they certainly don't hide what you own and where your properties are located.

It also informs your competition exactly what you are doing, and in what part of the city you found your sweet-spot for great real estate to flip. And if you hold real estate as a long-term
investment, as in rentals, you want even more privacy.

You will also learn:
How to conduct your own title searches
How to self-close your own transactions
How to create your own deeds and closing documents
How to file them yourself.

Who Needs This Book?
Wholesalers
Double Closers
Land Flippers
Landlords-Owners

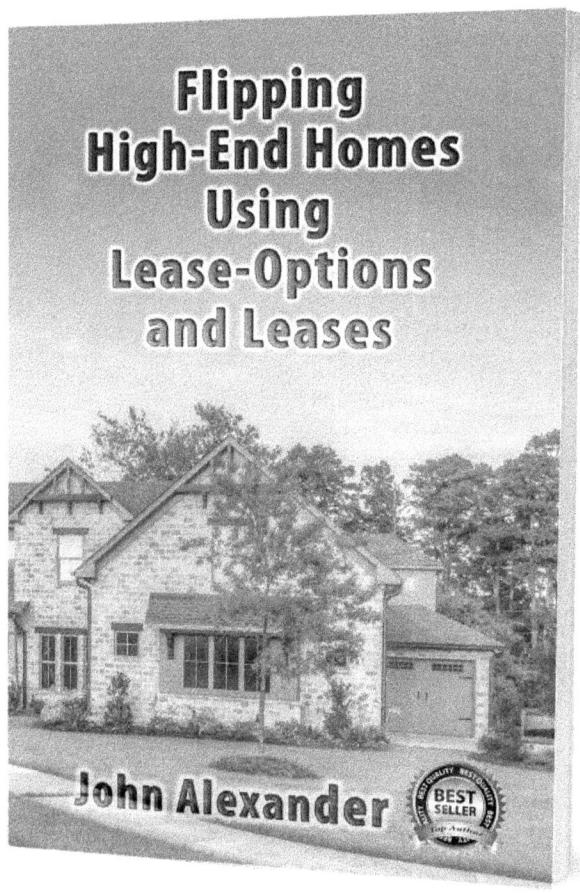

As the market climbs higher, money is starting to tighten. Higher-end homes slow down first. Here is the perfect cure to the problem happening right now in the market.

How it works:

You use our A-B option contract for this step. Seller is A, you are B. Once

[116]

contracted, you then will use our methods to release the home to a pre-qualified "Lease with Option to Buy" or "Lessee" party that has been approved using a proven pre-qualification process.

How to Discount Notes, How to buy Discounted Notes and how to Flip Discounted Notes. This is a complete course on how to run your own Discounted Note Brokering or Investing business.

You will learn every aspect of being a Discounted Note Broker in these pages, from my proven ways of finding unlimited notes -to using my mortgage purchase agreement (included) to locking in the flip to my list of favorite note wholesale buyers. They will buy almost any kind of payment stream, even newly created notes.

You will even learn how to buy and flip notes on auction sites. Single or bulk note purchases from small banks, to finding notes from online county deed records, it's all here, everything I've learned over 35 years in the note business.

This book is a course I sold for many years at prices from $300 to over $1000 in various seminar formats.

I have now made the information available in book form that anyone can afford. I keep it up to date so you know the methods in the latest edition is what is working right now in the discounted note industry.

This book is considered the Note Broker's Bible in the Discount Note Brokering and Note Investing industry for many years.

You will learn how to buy a full note, a partial note, partial payments, full balloon note, part of a balloon note, part of the monthly payment and part of any balloon. All done with both financial calculators and John's free online note broking calculators that make it super easy to create different offers depending on what the note holder needs.

New for 2018 is how the Dodd-Frank Act affects the note business and I reveal my favorite type of note to create, hold, and flip that doesn't fall under the Dodd-Frank regulations. Yet, it is one of the safest notes available today.

This note can be flipped to private investor or even Self-Directed IRA holders paying out a yield up to 20%.

I also share my top method for creating 20% to 30% yielding notes that you can keep or flip to investors and note buyers. These are rock solid, secure real estate notes that you can create on deals in your local area.

[119]

About the Author

John Alexander is an active real estate investor of over 30-years and a best-selling author. He has trained tens of thousands of real estate investors nationally since 1994. He has authored over 10 books on various real estate flipping techniques including the creation and publication of the Flex Option, The Inverse Purchase, and the Compound Deed flip methods, the Contract Release, as well as various creative note buying methods. His book "Millionaire Mind Programming" describes his rise from living on the streets as a homeless man to multi-millionaire and examines specific steps that anyone can use to program their mind for success.

www.JohnAlexander.com

www.ingramcontent.com/pod-product-compliance
Lightning Source LLC
Chambersburg PA
CBHW071706040426
42446CB00011B/1941